Enter Here
Beloved

Enter Here Beloved

by

HILARY BEE

THE CLOISTER HOUSE PRESS

First published in the United Kingdom in 2021 by
The Cloister House Press

ISBN 978-1-913460-39-6

Contents

These words are dedicated
to life.

Enter Here Beloved

enter here beloved
from the commands of time
step in
feet bare upon the earth
finding the sanctuary
that is yours, only yours

honouring the journey
with honest bread and water
tenderly opening
words tumble forth unbidden
intimacies admitting
heart reaching heart
we thirst to touch once more

The Sylkies

through all we've lost
and given away
we kept our songs
and the salt in our tears
and sometimes
in the light of the moon
ancient memories stir
keening us back
to our voluptuous freedom

our song is rising now
finding our way
to what was plundered
we slip back once more
into the skin we abandoned
leaving all behind
we return to the ocean
suddenly at home
in the depths
we had never forgotten

Did A Great Yearning

taking these seconds, weeks, years
taking these tastes, sounds, sights
weaving my wonder
at the benediction of life

did a great yearning
personal, in unison
allow me a turn
in this teaming field

jumping ecstatically
remembering nothing
into a florid affair
over when it's over

Trees Count

Tellingly, trees can count
carefully numbering successive warm days
before they unfurl their leaves

When did people stop counting trees
as elders, benefactors and friends
as essential as our breath?

immeasurable gratitude
infinite love
boundless awe
sacred covenant
join us together

Trees count
I bet my life on it

Boscawen-Un

circling rooks
and moss covered copse
guardians to Boscawen-Un
allowed us passage
over blossom strewn brook
till we made our own circles once more
weaving each stone
into a garland of sound
singing bowls honouring
our ceremony of care

Bright With Hope

bright with hope
patient with possibility
you lie in bliss
at my feet
pregnant, expectant
dear acorn

Twilight On The Dart

returning to the rhythm of the water
the river exhaling
the choir of trees at dusk
ducks scatter at my footfall
the wind wrestles the current
and I find myself here again
on the banks that have held me
through the tides of
these disconcerting years

Startled By A Poppy

startled by a poppy
arrestingly audacious
defiantly claiming
the carefully groomed bank
of a field just bulldozed
for a housing estate

your brilliant redness
displaying my outrage
with a plot named without irony
dandelion dell
covered with concrete
and only a poppy to protest

Alone

alone
of god's creatures
we wreak destruction
because we think
we are
alone

Still That Furtive Tent

still that furtive tent
amid the wild garlic
on the dogged riverbank
quietly zipped up
like my helplessness
stumbling against
your homelessness

Homs

proud city
bombed to indignity
where will your fabled
sense of humour
dispelled to desperate camps
shine again

White Prison

when did I forget
where I came from
when did I forget
who begat me
when did I forget
my colour

leeching out
every shade
we built
blinding walls

now I'm in
a pallid prison
stripped of my
humanity

a whited sepulchre

Until I Renounce

I won't take a shovel
to my sadness
as if there were an end
or a beginning

Instead I'll let her
wrap her arms around me
and croon in my ear

Or whip her storm
through my mortality
and cleave my bones

Or spread herself so thin
I can't fathom where
she begins or I end

Or summon me
unannounced from slumber
and leave me confounded

Or fade away unnoticed
until I renounce
she was my faithful lover

Ambushed By Grief

ambushed by grief
fault-lines fracture
no footing for my soul
pandemonium below the pleasantries
the genie won't go back

nothing to do
but concede

Child Of Mine

My child does not know how I fought for her
withheld sex from her father
and threatened to out him
until he coughed up for her care

> My child does not know how I fought for her
> kept the doctor from taking her
> quarantined myself with her
> and exercised her limbs back to life

My children do not know how I fought for them
protected their secrets
from well meaning colleagues
and betrayed my friendships for theirs

> My child does not know how I fought for her
> defied the abortion they pushed on me
> parted with her stoically
> and ache for her daily even now

> I brood that I can smell your skin
> and nuzzle your soft hair again
> you let me hold you through your pain
> as what came after falls away
> you see what I did for you
> as well as what I failed to do

> Let me not die
> apart from you
> child of mine
> come home to me

No Hiding Place

Shame was an acid attack
    still corroding my heart
Shame was a thief
    still devouring my goodness
Shame was an executioner
    still taking my life

Yet when love holds up her mirror
    shame has no face
    shame has no shadow
    shame has no hiding place

Only love remains

To Love Ourselves

Whose harsh relentless voice
have I taken as my own
castigating me so convincingly
I have no tongue nor breath

On my mother's mother's mother's
grave I pray
we are all set free
to love ourselves
in perpetuity

My Life Is Before Me

I have arisen
from my bed of depression
my children stripped from me
by juggernaut justice
I stand here unheard

I have arisen
from my bed of despair
my name defiled
by officials and friends
I stand here deserted

I have arisen
from my bed of inertia
my home long gone
my illusions discarded
I stand here transparent

I have arisen
from my bed of shame and anger
my actions ineffective
nor inactions either
I stand here disarmed

I have arisen
from my bed of loneliness
many have gone
I see who's beside me
simply I stand

I am rising
I am clear
I am beautiful
What can be taken has gone
What remains is priceless
I am thankful
I am forgiving
I am radiant
My life is before me

Three Years In Thrall

I was snatched in the night
from my deliberately childless bed
by a penetrating dream
that tore me clean away

No hair spared from recruitment
by this jealous dictator
demanding new life
and a legacy from my flesh

A stranger looking through my eyes
longing for only one unobtainable joy
beaten by my own blood
month after month after month

One day the unguarded doors must have yielded
for I find myself barefoot, transported
blinking in the loud sunlight
grateful, released, alive

Call Back To Life

Not so caught in activity now
That I forget the long void
Of rampant nullity

Not so completely lost then
That I couldn't come to feel
The call back to life

Mute On My Soapbox

on this magical land
loaned to me for a lifetime
how to keep my covenant
to speak for the wordless

how to convey utter awe
how to describe shimmering cobwebs
how to reveal unbounded reverence

I tremble
mute on my soapbox

Lighting Up The Night

from the darkness
come two men
selling flowers
"they're very fresh"

"we're just two homeless guys"
as I scramble for my change
one hands me a small bunch
the other wishes me
"the sweetest sweetest dreams"

"you too" I say
and walk away
tears falling for their innocence
and mine

home I arrange
my priceless bouquet
where it twinkles at me
lighting up the night

Robin On The Bike Path

tiny being calling me out
you hop on the fence
lock me right with your eye
engaging me across the worlds

you hold me mesmerised in liquid time
professor of presence
my to-do list in shreds
I cannot leave before you

suddenly you fly to me
an arrow to my heart
glancing my arm
then away

I am left quivering
at the power of your touch
your thrilling wing
dispensing words
fiercely spoken

We Opened The Box

we opened the box
wild forces unleashed
chaos confusion rage devastation
no winners all losers it seems

unless this is the birthplace
the long awaited cauldron
a reawakening
from stupor

let us tread with great respect
upon this holy hour

Pas De Deux

when you dance
with the abyss
let her lead
surrendering
to the rapture
of her rule

The Water Is Rising

the water is rising
again the swans make their nest
laid by heartbreaking habit
where year after year
the tide spoils their eggs

let us see the swelling waters
let us move to higher ground
let us build on the sureness
of our shared vitality
before we all drown

You Hold My Stone

you hold my stone
while I am gone

you hold my stone
as I sink below
as I unravel
and unbecome

you read the wind
you touch the earth
you hear the water
you tend the fire

you hold my stone
through vast days and nights
you hold my promise to return
my promise not to look behind
as I drag myself away
from scintillating mystery

you hold my stone
you witness my reassembly
my return to chronology
and the promises I made
to those who gifted me
with compelling generosity

you held my stone
till I came home

Homage In Minneapolis

on bended knee
we speak thy many names
we cannot sleep
till every life
of every colour and hue
is sacrosanct, inviolable
and thee is me
mine is thine
and all accorded
sacred sovereignty
on earth as they are in heaven

Dreaming Big For All Our Sakes

horizon to horizon
earth to sky
our most audacious dreams
are seeding now

This Is The Time

meditating on the canons
the signs have all appeared
they send one monk
to the highest summit

across the flimsy air
he draws his mallet
striking their gong
again and again and again

the attendant mountains
take up the tones
pulsing the rhythm
across continent and sea

to us all they say
wake up wake up
remember who you are
this is the time

Dhumavati's Chariot

everything precious to me is stolen
the great dissolution leaves me empty
i too dissolve

and as we become one life
our abandoned powers return

calling ancient remembrances
we spin threads from the sky
crafting a chariot
unfettered by space or time
birthing our destiny anew

Poetry

if my life
is my art
then this is
poetry

With deep gratitude to my sisters
Nicky Britten and Annie Lapaz
for helping me birth this collection.